Max Fortune

MASTERING THE ART OF REMOTE WORK

Strategies for Sustainable Success

Strategies For Productivity
And Success in the Digital
Age

MASTERING THE ART OF REMOTE WORK

Strategies for Productivity and Success in the Digital Age

By Max Fortune

Contact Information

Website: https://www.amazon.com/author/maxfortune2

Table of Contents

Introduction: The Rise of Remote Work

In the early 21st century, a seismic shift began to unfold in the way we approach work. Traditionally, work was synonymous with physical office space, a daily commute, and the confines of a structured 9-to-5 schedule. However, advancements in technology, coupled with changing cultural attitudes, have dramatically altered this paradigm. The rise of remote work has transformed the professional landscape, offering unprecedented flexibility and opportunities for both employers and employees.

The Evolution of Remote Work

The concept of remote work isn't entirely new. For decades, certain professions, particularly in fields like writing, consulting, and sales, have allowed for a degree of location independence. However, the true catalyst for widespread remote work came with the advent of high-speed internet, powerful personal computers, and a plethora of collaboration tools that made it possible to work virtually anywhere.

In the late 2000s and early 2010s, companies began to experiment more broadly with remote work policies. Tech giants like Google and Microsoft led the way, utilizing their products to enable remote work. Freelancing platforms such as Upwork and Fiverr further legitimized remote work by connecting businesses with a global talent pool.

The COVID-19 pandemic in 2020 acted as an unprecedented accelerant for remote work adoption. With lockdowns and social distancing measures in place, millions of workers worldwide were suddenly required to work from home. What was initially seen as a temporary measure revealed a profound truth: many jobs could be performed just as effectively outside the traditional office environment.

Why Remote Work is Here to Stay

The pandemic provided a global, large-scale proof of concept for remote work, leading to significant changes in workplace policies and employee expectations. Companies realized the cost savings associated with reduced office space and utilities, while employees embraced the flexibility and improved work-life balance that remote work offered.

Studies have shown that remote workers often report higher job satisfaction and increased productivity. Without the need for lengthy commutes, employees have more time for personal activities, family, and self-care, contributing to a healthier, more balanced lifestyle. Furthermore, remote work opens up job opportunities to individuals regardless of geographical location, fostering greater diversity and inclusion in the workforce.

Employers, too, benefit from the broader talent pool that remote work enables. Companies can now hire the best candidates from around the world, rather than being limited to those within commuting distance of a physical office. This has led to a more competitive and dynamic job market, with businesses vying to attract top talent with attractive remote work policies.

Benefits and Challenges of Remote Work

While remote work offers numerous benefits, it also presents unique challenges that must be addressed to ensure success. One of the primary advantages is flexibility. Employees can often set their schedules, which can lead to increased productivity and job satisfaction. This flexibility is particularly beneficial for those with family obligations or other personal commitments.

However, remote work requires a high degree of self-discipline and effective time management. Without the structure of a traditional office environment, it can be easy to become distracted or to blur the lines between work and personal time. This can lead to overworking and burnout if not managed carefully.

Communication is another critical aspect of remote work. In a traditional office, communication is often spontaneous and informal, occurring naturally throughout the day. In a remote work setting, however, communication must be more deliberate. This necessitates the use of various digital tools and platforms to facilitate collaboration and maintain team cohesion.

Moreover, remote work can sometimes lead to feelings of isolation and loneliness, particularly for individuals who thrive on social interaction. Building and maintaining relationships with colleagues can be more challenging when working remotely, making it essential for companies to foster a strong sense of community and support among remote teams.

Preparing for the Journey Ahead

This book, "Mastering the Art of Remote Work: Strategies for Productivity and Success in the Digital Age," is designed to serve as a comprehensive guide for navigating the remote work landscape. Whether you are an employee seeking to enhance your remote work experience, a manager striving to lead a distributed team, or an entrepreneur looking to build a remote-first company, this book offers practical advice, proven strategies, and valuable insights to help you succeed.

We will explore essential topics such as setting up an effective home office, mastering time management, utilizing communication tools, maintaining work-life balance, and overcoming common remote work challenges. Additionally, we will delve into advanced topics like cybersecurity, career development, and future trends in remote work.

By the end of this book, you will be equipped with the knowledge and skills necessary to thrive in a remote work environment. You will learn how to leverage the benefits of remote work while mitigating its challenges, ultimately achieving greater productivity, satisfaction, and success in your professional life.

Welcome to the future of work. Welcome to the world of remote work.

Setting Up Your Home Office: Essentials for Success

Creating an effective home office is crucial for remote work success. It involves thoughtful planning and investing in the right space, equipment, and ergonomic setup to ensure productivity, comfort, and well-being. This chapter will guide you through the process of establishing a home office that enhances your remote work experience.

Choosing the Right Space

Selecting the appropriate space for your home office is the first step toward a productive remote work environment. The ideal space should be quiet, free from distractions, and conducive to focused work. Here are some key considerations:

1. Location and Privacy: Choose a location in your home that offers privacy and minimizes interruptions. If possible, select a separate room with a door that can be closed to create a clear boundary between work and personal life. This separation helps signal to yourself and others that you are in work mode.

2. Natural Light: Aim to set up your workspace near a window to take advantage of natural light. Natural light can boost mood, reduce eye strain, and enhance overall well-being. However, be mindful of glare on your screen and adjust your desk position or use curtains and blinds as needed.

3. Quiet Environment: A quiet space is essential for maintaining focus and productivity. Avoid high-traffic areas of your home where noise and interruptions are common. If complete silence isn't possible, consider using noise-canceling headphones or a white noise machine to create a more conducive work environment.

4. Ventilation and Temperature Control: Ensure your workspace is well-ventilated and has appropriate temperature control. Fresh air and a comfortable temperature can significantly impact your comfort and ability to concentrate. Avoid areas that are too hot or cold, as extreme temperatures can be distracting.

Essential Equipment and Tools

Once you've chosen the right space, equipping your home office with the necessary tools and technology is the next step. Investing in quality equipment can enhance your efficiency and work experience. Here are the essentials:

1. Desk and Chair: A sturdy desk and an ergonomic chair are fundamental to your home office. Your desk should provide ample space for your computer, accessories, and any other work-related materials. An adjustable chair with good lumbar support is crucial for maintaining proper posture and reducing the risk of back pain.

2. Computer and Monitor: A reliable computer is the backbone of your remote work setup. Depending on your job requirements, you may need a desktop or laptop with sufficient processing power and memory. Additionally, consider using an external monitor to expand your screen real estate, which can boost productivity and reduce eye strain.

3. Keyboard and Mouse: Invest in a comfortable keyboard and mouse. Ergonomic options can help prevent repetitive strain injuries. A wireless keyboard and mouse can also reduce clutter and provide more flexibility in your workspace layout.

4. High-Speed Internet: A fast and stable internet connection is vital for remote work, especially for tasks that involve video conferencing, large file transfers, or online collaboration. Consider upgrading your internet plan if necessary and use a wired connection for added reliability.

5. Headphones and Microphone: Quality headphones with a built-in microphone or a separate headset are essential for clear communication during virtual meetings and calls. Noise-canceling headphones can also help you stay focused in a noisy environment.

6. Printer and Scanner: Depending on your work, you may need a printer and scanner for handling physical documents. Choose a reliable all-in-one printer that suits your needs and fits within your workspace.

7. Storage Solutions: Organize your workspace with storage solutions such as filing cabinets, shelves, and desk organizers. Keeping your area tidy and free from clutter can enhance focus and productivity.

Ergonomics and Comfort

Creating an ergonomic and comfortable workspace is essential for your health and well-being. Poor ergonomics can lead to discomfort, fatigue, and long-term health issues. Here are some tips to optimize your setup:

1. Desk Height and Monitor Placement: Ensure your desk is at a height that allows your arms to rest comfortably at a 90-degree angle while typing. Position your monitor at eye level, about 20-

30 inches away from your face, to avoid neck and eye strain. Use a monitor stand or adjustable desk to achieve the ideal height.

2. Chair Adjustments: Adjust your chair so that your feet are flat on the floor and your knees are at a 90-degree angle. The chair's backrest should support your lower back's natural curve. Consider using a footrest if needed to maintain proper posture.

3. Keyboard and Mouse Position: Place your keyboard and mouse close enough to avoid overreaching. Your wrists should be in a neutral position, not bent up or down. An ergonomic keyboard and mouse pad with wrist support can help maintain a comfortable position.

4. Lighting: In addition to natural light, ensure you have adequate task lighting. A desk lamp with adjustable brightness can reduce eye strain and create a well-lit workspace for reading and writing.

5. Breaks and Movement: Incorporate regular breaks and movement into your work routine to prevent fatigue and discomfort. Follow the 20-20-20 rule: every 20 minutes, take a 20-second break and look at something 20 feet away to rest your eyes. Stand up, stretch, and move around periodically to keep your body active.

6. Personal Comfort: Customize your workspace to suit your personal comfort preferences. Use a cushion or lumbar support pillow for added comfort in your chair. Keep a water bottle nearby to stay hydrated, and consider adding personal touches like plants or artwork to make your workspace more inviting.

By thoughtfully selecting your workspace, investing in essential equipment, and prioritizing ergonomics and comfort, you can create a home office that supports your productivity, health, and overall well-being. A well-designed home office not only enhances your work experience but also contributes to long-term success in a remote work environment.

Time Management: Strategies for a Structured Workday

Effective time management is a cornerstone of remote work success. Without the structure of a traditional office environment, it's essential to develop strategies that help you stay organized, focused, and productive. This chapter explores key techniques for creating a daily routine, prioritizing tasks, and avoiding procrastination, all of which contribute to a well-structured workday.

Creating a Daily Routine

Establishing a daily routine is crucial for maintaining a sense of normalcy and discipline in your remote work life. A consistent routine can help you transition into work mode, manage your time effectively, and achieve a healthy work-life balance. Here are some steps to create an effective daily routine:

1. Set a Regular Start Time: Begin your workday at the same time each day. This consistency helps regulate your internal clock and establishes a clear boundary between personal time and work time. Treat your remote work schedule as you would a traditional office job, waking up and getting ready as if you were commuting to an office.

2. Plan Your Day: Spend a few minutes each evening or first thing in the morning planning your day. Outline your tasks, meetings, and goals. This proactive approach allows you to start your day with a clear plan and reduces time spent deciding what to work on next.

3. Create Time Blocks: Divide your day into dedicated time blocks for specific tasks and activities. For example, allocate morning hours for focused work, midday for meetings or collaborative tasks, and afternoons for administrative work or creative projects. Time blocking helps you stay on track and ensures that all necessary tasks receive attention.

4. Include Breaks and Downtime: Schedule regular breaks to rest and recharge. Short breaks, such as five minutes or a quick walk, can boost your productivity and prevent burnout. Consider using the Pomodoro Technique, which involves working for 25 minutes followed by a five-minute break. Additionally, take a longer lunch break to relax and refuel.

5. Set a Clear End Time: Establish a consistent end time for your workday. This helps you maintain a work-life balance and prevents work from spilling into your time. Create a ritual to signal the end of your workday, such as shutting down your computer, tidying your workspace, or taking a short walk.

Prioritizing Tasks

Effective task prioritization ensures that you focus on the most important and urgent tasks first, maximizing your productivity and minimizing stress. Here are some strategies for prioritizing tasks:

1. Identify Key Tasks: Start by identifying your most critical tasks for the day. These are the tasks that have the highest impact on your goals or deadlines. Use a task management system, such as a to-do list or a digital planner, to keep track of your tasks.

2. Use the Eisenhower Matrix: The Eisenhower Matrix is a powerful tool for prioritizing tasks based on their urgency and importance. Divide your tasks into four categories:
    - Important and Urgent: Tasks that require immediate attention and have significant consequences if not completed.
    - Important but Not Urgent: Tasks that are important for long-term goals but do not require immediate action.
    - Urgent but Not Important: Tasks that need to be done quickly but have little impact on your long-term goals. Delegate these tasks if possible.
    - Not Urgent and Not Important: Tasks that have little value and can be minimized or eliminated.

3. Apply the 80/20 Rule: The Pareto Principle, or 80/20 Rule, suggests that 80% of your results come from 20% of your efforts. Identify the tasks that contribute the most to your goals and prioritize them. Focus on high-impact activities that drive significant progress.

4. Set SMART Goals: Ensure your tasks and goals are Specific, Measurable, Achievable, Relevant, and Time-bound (SMART). This clarity helps you stay focused and motivated. Break down larger goals into smaller, manageable tasks to make them more achievable.

5. Review and Adjust: Regularly review your task list and priorities. At the end of each day, evaluate your progress and adjust your plan for the next day. This continuous review helps you stay aligned with your goals and respond to changing priorities.

Avoiding Procrastination

Procrastination can be a significant barrier to productivity, especially in a remote work environment where distractions are plentiful. Here are some strategies to help you overcome procrastination:

1. Understand the Root Causes: Identify why you procrastinate. Common reasons include feeling overwhelmed by the task, fearing failure, lacking motivation, or being easily distracted. Understanding the root cause can help you address it more effectively.

2. Break Tasks into Smaller Steps: Large tasks can be daunting and lead to procrastination. Break them down into smaller, more manageable steps. Focus on completing one step at a time, which can make the task feel less overwhelming and more achievable.

3. Use the Two-Minute Rule: If a task takes less than two minutes to complete, do it immediately. This rule helps you tackle small tasks quickly and prevents them from piling up. It also builds momentum and encourages you to continue working on other tasks.

4. Set Clear Deadlines: Assign specific deadlines to your tasks, even if they are self-imposed. Deadlines create a sense of urgency and help you stay accountable. Use a calendar or task management tool to track your deadlines and progress.

5. Eliminate Distractions: Identify and eliminate distractions in your work environment. This may include turning off notifications, creating a dedicated workspace, or using website blockers to limit access to distracting websites. Set specific times to check email and social media to avoid constant interruptions.

6. Reward Yourself: Use positive reinforcement to motivate yourself. Set up a reward system for completing tasks or reaching milestones. Rewards can be small, such as taking a short break, enjoying a snack, or indulging in a favorite activity.

7. Practice Self-Compassion: Be kind to yourself if you procrastinate. Negative self-talk can increase stress and make it harder to get back on track. Instead, acknowledge your procrastination, understand why it happened, and refocus on your goals.

8. Use Accountability Partners: Share your goals and progress with a friend, colleague, or accountability partner. Regular check-ins can help you stay motivated and committed to your tasks. Knowing that someone else is aware of your goals can provide an extra layer of accountability.

By creating a structured daily routine, prioritizing tasks effectively, and implementing strategies to avoid procrastination, you can enhance your time management skills and achieve greater productivity in your remote work. These techniques will help you stay organized, focused, and motivated, leading to a more successful and fulfilling work experience.

Mindfulness and Focus Techniques

In addition to the strategies mentioned earlier, incorporating mindfulness and focus techniques into your daily routine can significantly reduce procrastination and enhance productivity. Here are some effective methods:

1. Mindfulness Meditation: Practicing mindfulness meditation can improve concentration and reduce stress. Spend a few minutes each day meditating, focusing on your breath, and bringing

your attention back whenever your mind wanders. This practice helps you stay present and better manage distractions.

2. Deep Work: Coined by Cal Newport, the concept of deep work involves dedicating uninterrupted time blocks to focus on cognitively demanding tasks. Schedule specific periods for deep work each day, during which you eliminate all distractions and immerse yourself in your work.

3. Pomodoro Technique: The Pomodoro Technique involves working for a set period (usually 25 minutes), followed by a short break (5 minutes). After four work sessions, take a longer break (15-30 minutes). This method helps maintain focus and prevent burnout by balancing work and rest.

4. Visualization: Visualize the successful completion of your tasks. Picture the steps you need to take and the positive outcomes that will result. Visualization can increase motivation and provide clarity on the actions required to achieve your goals.

5. Single-Tasking: Focus on one task at a time instead of multitasking. Multitasking can reduce efficiency and increase errors. Prioritize your tasks and work on them sequentially, giving each task your full attention.

Building Healthy Habits

Establishing healthy habits can support long-term productivity and reduce procrastination. Here are some habits to consider:

1. Consistent Sleep Schedule: Ensure you get enough sleep each night by maintaining a consistent sleep schedule. Quality sleep improves cognitive function, mood, and overall productivity. Aim for 7-9 hours of sleep per night.

2. Healthy Eating: Fuel your body and mind with nutritious foods. A balanced diet can enhance energy levels, concentration, and overall well-being. Avoid excessive caffeine and sugar, as they can lead to energy crashes.

3. Regular Exercise: Incorporate regular physical activity into your routine. Exercise boosts energy, reduces stress, and improves mental clarity. Find activities you enjoy, whether it's walking, yoga, or more intense workouts.

4. Hydration: Stay hydrated throughout the day. Dehydration can lead to fatigue and decreased cognitive performance. Keep a water bottle at your desk and set reminders to drink water regularly.

5. Work-Life Balance: Maintain a healthy work-life balance by setting boundaries between work and personal time. Engage in hobbies and activities outside of work to recharge and prevent burnout.

Tools and Resources

Leverage tools and resources to enhance your time management and productivity. Here are some recommendations:

1. Task Management Apps: Use task management apps like Todoist, Asana, or Trello to organize your tasks and projects. These apps allow you to create to-do lists, set deadlines, and track progress.

2. Calendar Tools: Utilize digital calendars like Google Calendar or Microsoft Outlook to schedule your tasks, meetings, and deadlines. Set reminders to stay on track and allocate time for focused work.

3. Focus Apps: Focus apps like Forest or Focus@Will can help you stay focused by minimizing distractions. Forest, for example, encourages you to stay off your phone by growing a virtual tree while you work.

4. Time Tracking: Track your time to understand how you spend your workday. Tools like Toggl or RescueTime can provide insights into your time usage and help identify areas for improvement.

Overcoming Common Procrastination Traps

Understanding common procrastination traps can help you avoid them. Here are some pitfalls to watch out for:

1. Perfectionism: Striving for perfection can lead to procrastination. Accept that perfection is unattainable and focus on progress instead. Aim for excellence, but recognize that mistakes and learning are part of the process.

2. Overwhelm: Feeling overwhelmed by the magnitude of a task can cause procrastination. Break tasks into smaller, manageable steps and tackle them one at a time. Celebrate small wins to maintain motivation.

3. Lack of Motivation: Identify what motivates you and leverage it. Set clear goals, visualize success, and remind yourself of the benefits of completing tasks. Sometimes, starting with a small, easy task can build momentum.

4. Fear of Failure: Fear of failure can paralyze action. Embrace a growth mindset and view challenges as opportunities to learn and grow. Remember that failure is a natural part of the learning process and does not define your worth.

5. Lack of Clarity: Unclear tasks can lead to procrastination. Ensure your goals and tasks are specific and actionable. If you're unsure where to start, take a few minutes to plan and outline the steps needed to complete the task.

Developing a Proactive Mindset

Adopting a proactive mindset can transform your approach to time management and productivity. Here's how to cultivate this mindset:

1. Take Initiative: Proactively identify tasks and opportunities that align with your goals. Don't wait for instructions; take the initiative to start projects and seek out new challenges.

2. Plan Ahead: Anticipate potential obstacles and plan accordingly. Prepare for meetings, set aside time for important tasks, and create contingency plans for unexpected events.

3. Stay Adaptable: Be flexible and adaptable to change. Remote work often requires adjusting plans and priorities. Embrace change as an opportunity to learn and grow.

4. Reflect and Improve: Regularly reflect on your work habits and identify areas for improvement. Set aside time for self-assessment and seek feedback from colleagues or mentors.

5. Celebrate Achievements: Acknowledge and celebrate your accomplishments, both big and small. Recognizing your achievements boosts motivation and reinforces positive habits.

By implementing these strategies and cultivating a proactive mindset, you can effectively manage your time, prioritize tasks, and overcome procrastination. These skills are essential for achieving a structured and productive workday, ultimately leading to greater success and fulfillment in your remote work journey.

Communication Tools: Staying Connected and Collaborative

Effective communication is fundamental to remote work success. Without the physical presence of colleagues, it is essential to leverage digital communication tools to stay connected, collaborative, and productive. This chapter delves into the various communication tools available, including video conferencing platforms, messaging, and collaboration tools, and outlines best practices for effective communication.

Video Conferencing Platforms

Video conferencing has become a cornerstone of remote work, enabling face-to-face interactions and fostering a sense of connection among distributed teams. Here are some of the most popular and effective video conferencing platforms:

1. Zoom: Zoom is one of the most widely used video conferencing platforms, known for its ease of use and robust feature set. It offers high-quality video and audio, screen sharing, breakout rooms, and recording capabilities. Zoom is suitable for both small team meetings and large webinars, making it a versatile choice for remote work.

2. Microsoft Teams: Integrated with the Microsoft 365 suite, Microsoft Teams is a comprehensive collaboration platform that includes video conferencing, chat, and file sharing. Teams allow for seamless integration with other Microsoft tools like Word, Excel, and OneNote, enhancing productivity and collaboration.

3. Google Meet: Part of the Google Workspace suite, Google Meet is a reliable video conferencing tool that integrates seamlessly with Google Calendar and Gmail. It offers features such as screen sharing, real-time captions, and the ability to join meetings directly from a browser without needing to download additional software.

4. Cisco Webex: Webex is a feature-rich video conferencing platform that provides high-definition video, audio, and content sharing. It includes advanced features like virtual backgrounds, noise cancellation, and AI-powered meeting insights. Webex is suitable for businesses of all sizes and industries.

5. Skype: Skype is a long-standing video conferencing tool that offers video calls, voice calls, messaging, and screen sharing. It is particularly useful for small teams or one-on-one meetings and can be accessed on various devices, including desktops, tablets, and smartphones.

Messaging and Collaboration Tools

In addition to video conferencing, effective remote work relies on messaging and collaboration tools that facilitate real-time communication and project management. Here are some essential tools:

1. Slack: Slack is a popular messaging platform designed for team communication and collaboration. It offers channels for organized discussions, direct messaging, and integration with numerous third-party apps. Slack's searchable message history and customizable notifications make it easy to stay on top of conversations and tasks.

2. Microsoft Teams: Beyond video conferencing, Microsoft Teams provides a comprehensive messaging and collaboration platform. Teams allow for threaded conversations, file sharing, and integration with Microsoft 365 applications. It also supports team and project management through channels and tabs.

3. Trello: Trello is a visual project management tool that uses boards, lists, and cards to help teams organize tasks and workflows. It is highly flexible and can be used for various types of projects, from simple to-do lists to complex project management. Trello integrates with many other tools, making it a versatile choice for remote teams.

4. Asana: Asana is a task and project management tool that helps teams plan, organize, and track work. It offers features such as task assignments, due dates, project timelines, and customizable workflows. Asana's visual interface and detailed reporting capabilities make it easy to manage projects and monitor progress.

5. Basecamp: Basecamp is a project management and team collaboration tool that combines to-do lists, file sharing, messaging, and scheduling in one platform. It is designed to simplify project management and improve team communication, making it a valuable tool for remote teams.

Effective Communication Practices

Using communication tools effectively requires more than just familiarity with the platforms. Adopting best practices for communication can enhance clarity, reduce misunderstandings, and foster a positive remote work culture. Here are some key practices:

1. Set Clear Expectations: Establish clear expectations for communication within your team. Define response times, preferred communication channels, and availability. For example, specify when to use email versus instant messaging and set boundaries for after-hours communication to maintain work-life balance.

2. Maintain Regular Check-Ins: Schedule regular check-ins with your team to discuss progress, address challenges, and provide updates. Weekly team meetings, one-on-one sessions, and daily stand-ups can help keep everyone aligned and ensure that any issues are promptly addressed.

3. Be Clear and Concise: When communicating remotely, clarity is crucial. Be clear and concise in your messages to avoid misunderstandings. Use bullet points, headers, and numbered lists to organize information, and provide context when necessary.

4. Use Video When Possible: Video calls can significantly enhance communication by allowing participants to see facial expressions and body language. Whenever possible, opt for video meetings over audio-only calls to foster better connections and understanding among team members.

5. Encourage Open Communication: Foster a culture of open communication where team members feel comfortable sharing ideas, asking questions, and providing feedback. Encourage active participation in meetings and create an inclusive environment where everyone's voice is heard.

6. Document and Share Information: Ensure that important information is documented and easily accessible. Use shared documents, wikis, or project management tools to store meeting notes, project plans, and guidelines. This practice helps prevent information silos and ensures that all team members have access to the same information.

7. Leverage Collaboration Features: Take full advantage of the collaboration features offered by your communication tools. Use shared documents for real-time collaboration, assign tasks within project management tools, and integrate apps to streamline workflows. These features can enhance efficiency and improve team coordination.

8. Provide Training and Support: Ensure that all team members are proficient in using the communication tools and platforms. Provide training sessions, tutorials, and ongoing support to help everyone navigate the tools effectively. Regularly update your team on new features and best practices.

Enhancing Remote Team Collaboration

Effective communication is the foundation of successful remote team collaboration. Here are additional strategies to enhance collaboration among remote teams:

1. Virtual Team Building: Invest time in virtual team-building activities to strengthen relationships and build trust among team members. Activities such as virtual coffee breaks, online games, and team challenges can create a sense of camaraderie and improve team dynamics.

2. Cross-Functional Collaboration: Encourage cross-functional collaboration by bringing together team members from different departments or expertise areas. This can lead to innovative solutions and a broader perspective on projects. Use communication tools to facilitate cross-functional meetings and brainstorming sessions.

3. Transparency and Accountability: Promote transparency and accountability by clearly defining roles, responsibilities, and project goals. Use project management tools to assign tasks, track progress, and provide visibility into each team member's contributions. Regularly update project status and celebrate milestones.

4. Feedback and Continuous Improvement: Establish a feedback loop to continuously improve communication and collaboration processes. Encourage team members to provide constructive feedback on meetings, workflows, and tools. Use this feedback to make adjustments and enhance team productivity.

5. Cultural Sensitivity: Be mindful of cultural differences and time zones when working with a diverse remote team. Respect varying communication styles, holidays, and work hours. Foster an inclusive environment where cultural diversity is celebrated, and all team members feel valued.

Future Trends in Remote Communication

As remote work continues to evolve, new trends and technologies are shaping the future of communication. Here are some emerging trends to watch:

1. Artificial Intelligence (AI) Integration: AI-powered tools are becoming increasingly prevalent in communication platforms. AI can assist with tasks such as scheduling meetings, transcribing calls, and providing real-time language translation. These advancements can enhance efficiency and accessibility in remote communication.

2. Virtual and Augmented Reality (VR/AR): VR and AR technologies are poised to revolutionize remote collaboration by creating immersive virtual environments. These technologies can enable virtual meetings, training sessions, and collaborative workspaces that mimic physical presence, enhancing the sense of connection among remote teams.

3. Unified Communication Platforms: The future of remote work may see the rise of unified communication platforms that integrate various communication tools into a single interface. This integration can streamline workflows, reduce tool fatigue, and provide a seamless communication experience.

4. Increased Focus on Cybersecurity: As remote work continues to grow, ensuring the security of communication tools and data is paramount. Future trends will likely include enhanced cybersecurity measures, such as end-to-end encryption, secure access controls, and robust authentication protocols.

5. Enhanced Analytics and Insights: Communication tools will increasingly offer advanced analytics and insights to help teams understand their communication patterns and improve efficiency. These insights can inform decisions on meeting frequency, collaboration practices, and tool usage.

By understanding and leveraging the various communication tools available, implementing effective communication practices, and staying informed about future trends, remote teams can stay connected, collaborative, and productive. Effective communication is the key to overcoming the challenges of remote work and achieving long-term success in a distributed work environment.

Work-Life Balance: Maintaining Boundaries in a Remote Environment

Achieving a healthy work-life balance is critical for maintaining well-being and productivity, especially in a remote work environment. Without the physical separation of an office, the lines between work and personal life can easily blur, leading to increased stress and burnout. This chapter explores strategies for setting boundaries with family and friends, taking breaks to avoid burnout, and creating a sustainable work-life balance.

Setting Boundaries with Family and Friends

One of the most significant challenges of remote work is managing interruptions and distractions from family and friends. Clear communication and established boundaries are essential to create a productive work environment at home. Here are some strategies:

1. Communicate Your Schedule: Communicate your work schedule to family and friends. Let them know your working hours and when you are available for personal interactions. Consider posting your schedule in a visible place or using a shared calendar to keep everyone informed.

2. Create a Dedicated Workspace: Designate a specific area in your home as your workspace. This physical boundary signals to others that you are in work mode and helps minimize interruptions. Ensure your workspace is equipped with everything you need to work efficiently and make it off-limits during work hours.

3. Establish House Rules: Set house rules for when you are working. For example, establish quiet hours during your work periods or ask family members to knock before entering your workspace. Consistency in enforcing these rules helps everyone adjust to their work routine.

4. Use Visual Cues: Visual cues can be effective in signaling your availability. Consider using a "do not disturb" sign on your door or a specific indicator, like wearing headphones, to show when you are focused on work. Conversely, have a different visual cue to indicate when you are available for personal interactions.

5. Schedule Quality Time: To prevent feelings of neglect among family and friends, schedule quality time with them outside of your work hours. This dedicated time ensures you maintain strong relationships while respecting your work boundaries.

6. Be Firm but Flexible: While it's important to be firm about your work boundaries, flexibility is also necessary. Understand that occasional interruptions are inevitable, especially in

households with children. Balance firmness with empathy and be willing to adjust your approach as needed.

Taking Breaks and Avoiding Burnout

Taking regular breaks is essential for maintaining mental and physical health. Without the natural breaks that occur in an office setting, remote workers need to be proactive in scheduling downtime to avoid burnout. Here are some effective strategies:

1. Follow a Break Schedule: Implement a structured break schedule, such as the Pomodoro Technique, which involves working for 25 minutes and then taking a 5-minute break. After four work intervals, take a longer break of 15-30 minutes. This approach helps maintain focus and prevent fatigue.

2. Incorporate Movement: Use breaks to incorporate physical activity into your day. Simple activities like stretching, walking, or doing a quick workout can boost your energy levels and reduce stress. Regular movement also helps counteract the sedentary nature of remote work.

3. Step Outside Whenever possible, step outside for fresh air and natural light during your breaks. Spending time outdoors can improve mood, enhance creativity, and provide a mental reset. Even a short walk around the block can have significant benefits.

4. Disconnect Completely: Ensure your brakes are true breaks by disconnecting from work-related activities. Avoid checking emails, taking work calls, or engaging in tasks that require cognitive effort. Use this time to relax and recharge, whether through reading, listening to music, or practicing mindfulness.

5. Set Boundaries with Technology: Set boundaries with technology to prevent burnout. Avoid constant connectivity by turning off work notifications during non-work hours and setting specific times to check emails. Create a digital detox routine to reduce screen time and enhance mental well-being.

6. Listen to Your Body: Pay attention to your body's signals and take breaks as needed. If you feel fatigued or stressed, allow yourself time to rest and recover. Overworking can lead to decreased productivity and long-term health issues, so prioritize self-care.

Creating a Healthy Work-Life Balance

A healthy work-life balance involves more than just managing work and personal time; it encompasses overall well-being and satisfaction in both areas. Here are strategies to create and maintain a balanced lifestyle:

1. Define Your Boundaries: Clearly define the boundaries between work and personal life. Establish specific start and end times for your workday and stick to them. Avoid letting work spill

over into your time and vice versa. This separation helps you fully engage in each aspect of your life.

2. Prioritize Self-Care: Make self-care a non-negotiable part of your routine. Incorporate activities that promote physical, mental, and emotional well-being, such as exercise, meditation, hobbies, and socializing. Prioritizing self-care enhances your overall quality of life and resilience.

3. Plan and Organize: Effective planning and organization are key to balancing work and personal responsibilities. Use calendars, to-do lists, and time management tools to schedule tasks and commitments. Plan your day, including work tasks, personal activities, and downtime.

4. Set Realistic Goals: Set realistic and achievable goals for both work and personal life. Break larger goals into smaller, manageable steps and celebrate your progress. Avoid overcommitting or setting unattainable expectations, which can lead to stress and burnout.

5. Create Rituals and Routines: Establish rituals and routines that signal transitions between work and personal time. For example, create a morning routine that prepares you for work and an evening routine that helps you unwind. These rituals can include activities like exercising, reading, or spending time with family.

6. Seek Support: Don't hesitate to seek support from family, friends, or colleagues. Share your challenges and successes, and be open to advice and assistance. Joining remote work communities or support groups can also provide valuable insights and encouragement.

7. Set Aside Personal Time: Dedicate time for personal interests and passions. Engage in activities that bring you joy and fulfillment outside of work. Whether it's pursuing a hobby, learning a new skill, or spending time with loved ones, personal time is essential for a balanced life.

8. Reflect and Adjust: Regularly reflect on your work-life balance and make adjustments as needed. Assess what's working and what's not, and be willing to make changes to improve your well-being. Flexibility and adaptability are crucial for maintaining balance in a dynamic remote work environment.

Leveraging Technology for Work-Life Balance

Technology, while often a source of distraction, can also be a valuable ally in maintaining work-life balance. Here are ways to leverage technology effectively:

1. Use Productivity Apps: Utilize productivity apps like Todoist, Asana, or Trello to organize tasks and manage time efficiently. These apps help you prioritize tasks, set deadlines, and track progress, allowing for better time management and reduced stress.

2. Set Digital Boundaries: Use apps and tools to set digital boundaries. Tools like Focus@Will or Freedom can block distracting websites and apps during work hours. Set up Do Not Disturb modes on your devices to minimize interruptions during personal time.

3. Automate Routine Tasks: Automate routine tasks using tools like IFTTT (If This Then That) or Zapier. Automation can save time and reduce the cognitive load associated with repetitive tasks, allowing you to focus on more important activities.

4. Track Screen Time: Monitor and manage your screen time using apps like Screen Time for iOS or Digital Wellbeing for Android. Set limits on the amount of time spent on non-essential apps and activities to reduce screen fatigue and improve overall well-being.

5. Leverage Health and Wellness Apps: Use health and wellness apps to support your self-care routine. Apps like Headspace or Calm offer guided meditation, while fitness apps like Nike Training Club or MyFitnessPal can help you stay active and healthy.

Overcoming Work-Life Balance Challenges

Achieving work-life balance in a remote environment comes with unique challenges. Here are some common challenges and strategies to overcome them:

1. Blurring of Boundaries: The lack of physical separation between work and home can blur boundaries. To counter this, create distinct physical and mental boundaries for work and personal time. Designate a specific workspace and establish clear start and end times for your workday.

2. Isolation and Loneliness: Remote work can lead to feelings of isolation and loneliness. Combat this by staying connected with colleagues and loved ones. Schedule regular virtual meetings, engage in online communities, and make time for social interactions.

3. Overworking: The flexibility of remote work can sometimes lead to overworking. Set strict boundaries for work hours and take regular breaks. Use time management techniques and tools to stay on track and avoid overextending yourself.

4. Distractions: Managing distractions at home can be challenging. Identify your biggest distractions and take steps to minimize them. Create a dedicated workspace, set house rules, and use productivity tools to stay focused.

5. Guilt and Pressure: Remote workers often feel guilty about not being constantly available or productive. Recognize that taking breaks and setting boundaries is essential for long-term productivity and well-being. Communicate openly with your employer and colleagues about your work patterns and needs.

By implementing these strategies, setting clear boundaries, taking regular breaks, and creating a healthy work-life balance, remote workers can thrive in their professional and personal lives. Maintaining balance requires ongoing effort and self-awareness, but the rewards are well worth it—a fulfilling and sustainable remote work experience.

Productivity Hacks: Techniques to Maximize Efficiency

Productivity is essential for success in any work environment, but it becomes especially crucial when working remotely. Without the structure of a traditional office, remote workers must employ effective strategies to manage their time and tasks efficiently. This chapter explores several productivity hacks, including time blocking and scheduling, the Pomodoro Technique, and minimizing distractions. These techniques can help maximize efficiency and ensure that you stay on top of your work.

Time Blocking and Scheduling

Time blocking and scheduling are powerful techniques for managing your workday. By allocating specific time blocks for different tasks and activities, you can ensure that you stay focused and productive. Here's a comprehensive look at how to effectively implement these strategies:

1. Identify Priorities: Start by identifying your priorities and the tasks that need to be accomplished. Break down your work into manageable chunks and categorize them by importance and urgency. This helps you understand what needs to be done first and allocate your time accordingly.

2. Create a Master Schedule: Develop a master schedule that outlines your daily, weekly, and monthly tasks. Use a digital calendar, planner, or time management app to create your schedule. Include all work-related activities, personal commitments, and breaks to get a complete overview of your time.

3. Allocate Time Blocks: Divide your day into time blocks dedicated to specific tasks or categories of tasks. For example, you might allocate the first hour of your workday to emails and administrative tasks, followed by a two-hour block for focused work on a key project. Be realistic about how much time each task requires and leave some buffer time between blocks.

4. Prioritize Deep Work: Reserve time blocks for deep work—tasks that require intense focus and cognitive effort. Schedule these blocks during your peak productivity periods, which may vary from person to person. Minimizing interruptions during these times is crucial for maintaining concentration and achieving high-quality work.

5. Include Breaks and Downtime: Incorporate regular breaks into your schedule to prevent burnout and maintain energy levels. Short breaks between time blocks and longer breaks for

meals or physical activity can significantly enhance productivity. Remember to schedule downtime and personal activities to maintain a healthy work-life balance.

6. Review and Adjust: Regularly review your schedule to assess its effectiveness. Reflect on what's working and what's not, and make necessary adjustments. Flexibility is key—adapt your schedule as priorities shift or unexpected tasks arise. Continuous improvement will help you refine your time-blocking and scheduling approach.

The Pomodoro Technique

The Pomodoro Technique is a time management method developed by Francesco Cirillo in the late 1980s. Named after the tomato-shaped kitchen timer he used, this technique breaks work into intervals, traditionally 25 minutes in length, separated by short breaks. Here's how to implement the Pomodoro Technique effectively:

1. Choose a Task: Select a specific task you want to work on. It can be anything from writing a report to coding a software program. The key is to focus on one task at a time.

2. Set a Timer: Set a timer for 25 minutes, known as one Pomodoro. During this time, concentrate solely on the task at hand. Avoid all distractions and interruptions. If you think of something else that needs attention, jot it down and return to it later.

3. Work Intensively: Work diligently for the entire 25 minutes. The goal is to immerse yourself in the task without letting your attention wander. This intense focus can lead to higher productivity and a greater sense of accomplishment.

4. Take a Short Break: When the timer goes off, take a short break of 5 minutes. Use this time to relax, stretch, or do something enjoyable. Stepping away from your work helps refresh your mind and prepares you for the next Pomodoro.

5. Repeat the Process: After the break, set the timer for another 25 minutes and repeat the process. Aim to complete four Pomodoros before taking a longer break of 15-30 minutes. This longer break allows for a more substantial rest and helps prevent burnout.

6. Track Your Progress: Keep track of how many Pomodoros you complete each day and use this information to analyze your productivity patterns. Tracking your progress can provide insights into how much time you need for various tasks and help you plan future work more effectively.

Minimizing Distractions

Minimizing distractions is crucial for maintaining focus and productivity, especially in a remote work environment where interruptions can be frequent. Here are comprehensive strategies to minimize distractions and create a more focused work environment:

1. Create a Distraction-Free Workspace: Set up a dedicated workspace that is free from distractions. Choose a quiet area of your home where you can work without interruptions. Keep your workspace organized and clutter-free to promote concentration and efficiency.

2. Use Noise-Canceling Tools: Invest in noise-canceling headphones or use white noise apps to block out background noise. Ambient noise or music can also help you focus, depending on your preference. Find the auditory environment that works best for you.

3. Set Boundaries: Communicate your work hours and boundaries to family members, roommates, or anyone you live with. Use visual cues, like a closed door or a "do not disturb" sign, to signal when you are working and should not be interrupted.

4. Limit Digital Distractions: Digital distractions, such as social media, emails, and notifications, can significantly hinder productivity. Use apps and browser extensions that block distracting websites during work hours. Set specific times to check emails and messages, rather than constantly monitoring them.

5. Turn Off Notifications: Disable non-essential notifications on your devices. This includes notifications from social media, news apps, and even some work-related apps that can interrupt your focus. Allow only critical notifications to come through.

6. Establish a Routine: A consistent routine can help minimize distractions and maintain focus. Start your day with a clear plan and stick to a structured schedule. Routine creates a sense of discipline and reduces the likelihood of getting sidetracked.

7. Practice Mindfulness: Incorporate mindfulness practices into your daily routine to enhance focus and reduce susceptibility to distractions. Techniques such as meditation, deep breathing, and mindfulness exercises can improve your ability to stay present and concentrated.

8. Use Focus Techniques: Employ focus techniques such as the Pomodoro Technique (discussed earlier), time blocking, or single-tasking. These methods encourage short bursts of focused work followed by breaks, helping to maintain high levels of productivity.

9. Manage Multitasking: Avoid multitasking, as it can lead to decreased efficiency and increased errors. Focus on completing one task at a time before moving on to the next. Prioritize tasks and handle them sequentially to maintain clarity and productivity.

10. Create a Distraction List: Keep a list of distractions that come to mind while you are working. Write down any non-urgent thoughts, tasks, or ideas that pop up, and address them during breaks or after work. This helps you stay focused without forgetting important items.

Enhancing Overall Productivity

In addition to the specific techniques mentioned, there are general practices that can further enhance productivity in a remote work environment:

1. Set Clear Goals: Define clear, achievable goals for each day, week, and month. Having specific targets helps you stay focused and motivated. Break larger goals into smaller, actionable steps to make them more manageable.

2. Prioritize Tasks: Prioritize your tasks based on importance and urgency. Use frameworks like the Eisenhower Matrix to categorize tasks and focus on what truly matters. Tackle high-priority tasks first to ensure critical work gets done.

3. Use Productivity Tools: Leverage productivity tools and apps to streamline your workflow. Tools like Trello, Asana, and Todoist can help you organize tasks, set deadlines, and track progress. Explore different tools to find the ones that best suit your needs.

4. Maintain Work-Life Balance: Ensure you maintain a healthy work-life balance by setting boundaries between work and personal time. Avoid overworking and schedule regular breaks and downtime. A balanced lifestyle enhances overall productivity and well-being.

5. Stay Organized: Keep your workspace and digital files organized. An organized environment reduces stress and saves time, making it easier to find what you need and stay focused on your work.

6. Seek Feedback and Reflect: Regularly seek feedback from colleagues, supervisors, or clients to identify areas for improvement. Reflect on your work habits and productivity strategies, and be open to making adjustments. Continuous learning and improvement are key to sustained productivity.

By implementing these productivity hacks and creating a structured, focused work environment, remote workers can maximize their efficiency and achieve their goals more effectively. These techniques not only enhance productivity but also contribute to a more satisfying and balanced work experience.

Overcoming Remote Work Challenges: Common Pitfalls and Solutions

Remote work offers flexibility and autonomy, but it also presents unique challenges that can impact productivity and well-being. This chapter addresses common pitfalls faced by remote workers, including dealing with isolation and loneliness, managing technical issues, and staying motivated. By understanding these challenges and implementing effective solutions, remote workers can thrive in their professional roles.

Dealing with Isolation and Loneliness

Remote work can lead to feelings of isolation and loneliness due to the lack of face-to-face interaction with colleagues. These feelings can impact mental health and overall job satisfaction. Here are strategies to combat isolation and foster a sense of connection:

1. Establish Regular Communication: Maintain regular communication with colleagues through virtual meetings, instant messaging platforms, and email. Schedule regular check-ins with your team to discuss projects, share updates, and socialize.

2. Participate in Virtual Events: Engage in virtual team-building activities, such as online happy hours, virtual coffee breaks, or team challenges. These activities promote camaraderie and strengthen relationships with remote colleagues.

3. Join Online Communities: Participate in online communities or professional networks related to your industry. Platforms like LinkedIn groups, Slack channels, or industry forums provide opportunities to connect with like-minded professionals and share experiences.

4. Seek Social Interactions: Schedule virtual lunches or coffee chats with coworkers to replicate informal office interactions. Use video conferencing tools to have face-to-face conversations and build personal connections.

5. Connect with Local Networks: Explore local networking groups or meetups for remote workers in your area. These events offer opportunities to meet new people, exchange ideas, and combat feelings of isolation.

6. Practice Self-Care: Prioritize self-care activities that promote mental well-being, such as exercise, meditation, hobbies, or spending time outdoors. Taking care of your emotional health is crucial for managing feelings of isolation.

7. Seek Support: If feelings of loneliness persist, reach out to friends, family members, or a mental health professional for support. Discussing your feelings with others can provide perspective and help you develop coping strategies.

Managing Technical Issues

Technical issues can disrupt workflow and productivity in a remote work environment. Whether it's connectivity problems, software glitches, or hardware malfunctions, addressing technical issues promptly is essential. Here's how to manage technical challenges effectively:

1. Ensure Reliable Internet Connection: Invest in a reliable internet connection with sufficient bandwidth for video conferencing and file sharing. Consider using a wired connection for stability, especially during critical meetings or deadlines.

2. Use Reliable Technology Tools: Choose reliable technology tools and software that are compatible with your workflow. Test new tools before implementation and ensure they meet your communication and collaboration needs.

3. Have Backup Plans: Develop contingency plans for common technical issues, such as power outages or internet disruptions. Keep backup devices, chargers, and cables readily available to minimize downtime.

4. Stay Updated: Regularly update software applications, operating systems, and antivirus programs to ensure they are secure and functioning optimally. Set automatic updates where possible to stay protected against vulnerabilities.

5. Troubleshoot Proactively: Learn basic troubleshooting techniques to resolve common technical problems independently. Familiarize yourself with software settings, internet troubleshooting steps, and device configurations.

6. Contact Technical Support: When encountering complex technical issues, contact technical support services provided by your company, software vendors, or internet service provider. Document error messages and steps taken for faster resolution.

7. Maintain Data Security: Practice good cybersecurity habits to protect sensitive information and prevent data breaches. Use strong passwords, enable two-factor authentication, and avoid accessing work-related content on public Wi-Fi networks.

Staying Motivated

Maintaining motivation can be challenging when working remotely, as it requires self-discipline and focus without direct supervision. Here are strategies to stay motivated and productive:

1. Set Clear Goals: Establish specific, achievable goals for your workday, week, and month. Break larger goals into smaller, actionable tasks to maintain momentum and track progress.

2. Create a Routine: Develop a daily routine that includes regular work hours, breaks, and activities that help you transition between work and personal time. Consistency in your schedule fosters productivity and discipline.

3. Use Task Management Tools: Utilize task management tools like Trello, Asana, or Todoist to organize tasks, set deadlines, and prioritize work. These tools help you stay focused and accountable for your assignments.

4. Practice Time Management: Implement time management techniques, such as time blocking or the Pomodoro Technique, to structure your workday effectively. Allocate focused time for tasks and schedule breaks to recharge.

5. Reward Progress: Celebrate small victories and milestones to maintain motivation. Acknowledge your achievements, whether it's completing a project milestone or mastering a new skill. Rewarding progress reinforces positive behavior.

6. Stay Connected: Engage with colleagues, mentors, or industry peers through virtual meetings, networking events, or professional development opportunities. Collaborate on projects, seek feedback, and stay connected to the broader work community.

7. Seek Learning Opportunities: Pursue learning and professional development to stay motivated and expand your skills. Take online courses, attend webinars, or participate in workshops related to your field of expertise.

8. Stay Healthy: Prioritize physical and mental well-being through regular exercise, healthy eating, and adequate sleep. Physical health directly impacts mental clarity and overall motivation. Incorporate wellness activities into your daily routine.

9. Set Boundaries: Establish boundaries between work and personal life to prevent burnout and maintain motivation. Define clear start and end times for your workday, and avoid overworking beyond scheduled hours.

10. Reflect and Adjust: Regularly assess your motivation levels and productivity strategies. Reflect on what motivates you, identify barriers, and make adjustments to your approach as needed. Continuous improvement enhances resilience and adaptability.

Conclusion

By addressing common pitfalls such as isolation and loneliness, managing technical issues effectively, and staying motivated, remote workers can overcome challenges and thrive in their professional roles. Implementing these strategies promotes productivity, enhances well-being, and fosters a positive remote work experience. With proactive approaches and a focus on personal development, remote workers can navigate challenges successfully and achieve their professional goals.

Mental Health: Staying Positive and Focused While Working Remotely

Maintaining mental health is crucial for remote workers to stay positive, focused, and productive. Working in isolation can present unique challenges that impact overall well-being. This chapter explores strategies for practicing mindfulness and meditation, seeking support and counseling, and maintaining physical health to promote mental well-being while working remotely.

Practicing Mindfulness and Meditation

Mindfulness and meditation practices can help remote workers reduce stress, enhance focus, and cultivate a positive mindset. Here's how to integrate these practices into your daily routine:

1. Start with Breathing Exercises: Begin your day with deep breathing exercises to center yourself and calm your mind. Focus on slow, deliberate breaths to reduce tension and promote relaxation.

2. Practice Mindful Awareness: Incorporate mindfulness into daily activities by staying present and aware of your thoughts, emotions, and surroundings. Pay attention to the sensations of work and take short breaks to reset.

3. Integrate Meditation Sessions: Set aside dedicated time for meditation sessions, even if it's just 5-10 minutes a day. Find a quiet space, sit comfortably, and focus on your breath or a guided meditation to clear your mind and reduce stress.

4. Use Mindfulness Apps: Explore mindfulness apps like Headspace, Calm, or Insight Timer for guided meditation sessions and mindfulness exercises. These apps offer resources to support your mental well-being and cultivate mindfulness habits.

5. Practice Gratitude: Cultivate a positive outlook by practicing gratitude daily. Reflect on things you're grateful for in your work and personal life. Keeping a gratitude journal can help you maintain perspective and enhance your overall mood.

6. Stay Present During Work Tasks: Focus fully on one task at a time and avoid multitasking. Mindful work habits improve concentration and productivity, leading to a sense of accomplishment and reduced stress.

7. Take Mindful Breaks: Incorporate mindful breaks throughout your workday to recharge. Step away from your workspace, stretch, or go for a short walk. Use this time to clear your mind and return to work with renewed focus.

Seeking Support and Counseling

Remote work can sometimes feel isolating, making it essential to seek support when needed. Here are ways to access support and counseling resources:

1. Utilize Employee Assistance Programs (EAP): Many employers offer EAP services that provide confidential counseling and support for employees. Take advantage of these resources to discuss work-related stress, mental health concerns, or personal challenges.

2. Engage with Mental Health Professionals: Consider scheduling virtual sessions with a licensed therapist or counselor. Virtual counseling services offer flexibility and convenience for remote workers seeking professional support.

3. Join Online Support Groups: Connect with online support groups or communities for remote workers or individuals facing similar challenges. These groups provide a platform to share experiences, receive advice, and find solidarity.

4. Reach Out to Colleagues and Friends: Maintain connections with colleagues, friends, and family members to discuss feelings of stress or loneliness. Sometimes, simply talking about your experiences can provide relief and perspective.

5. Participate in Wellness Programs: Participate in employer-sponsored wellness programs that promote mental health and well-being. These programs may include workshops, seminars, or resources on stress management and resilience.

6. Educate Yourself on Mental Health: Educate yourself about mental health issues, coping strategies, and self-care practices. Understanding mental health can help you recognize signs of distress and take proactive steps to maintain well-being.

7. Prioritize Self-Compassion: Be kind to yourself and recognize that it's okay to seek help when needed. Practice self-compassion by treating yourself with understanding and acceptance during challenging times.

Maintaining Physical Health

Physical health plays a significant role in supporting mental well-being. Incorporate these practices into your routine to stay physically healthy while working remotely:

1. Establish a Regular Exercise Routine: Schedule regular physical activity into your daily routine, such as home workouts, yoga sessions, or outdoor walks. Exercise releases endorphins, reduces stress, and boosts overall mood.

2. Take Breaks for Movement: Incorporate movement breaks throughout your workday to combat sedentary behavior. Stretch, walk around your home or neighborhood, or do brief exercises to improve circulation and energy levels.

3. Prioritize Healthy Nutrition: Maintain a balanced diet rich in fruits, vegetables, lean proteins, and whole grains. Avoid excessive caffeine and sugary snacks that can contribute to energy crashes and mood fluctuations.

4. Stay Hydrated: Drink plenty of water throughout the day to stay hydrated and maintain cognitive function. Dehydration can lead to fatigue and decreased concentration, impacting productivity.

5. Get Sufficient Sleep: Establish a consistent sleep schedule and aim for 7-9 hours of quality sleep each night. A restful sleep environment and bedtime routine can improve sleep quality and overall well-being.

6. Practice Ergonomic Work Habits: Set up an ergonomic workspace to promote physical comfort and reduce strain. Use an adjustable chair, position your monitor at eye level, and take frequent breaks to prevent repetitive stress injuries.

7. Limit Screen Time: Balance screen time by taking regular breaks to rest your eyes and reduce digital fatigue. Use blue light filters on devices and adjust screen brightness for optimal viewing comfort.

Conclusion

By prioritizing mental health through mindfulness and meditation practices, seeking support when needed, and maintaining physical well-being, remote workers can foster a positive and focused mindset. These strategies empower individuals to navigate challenges effectively, enhance resilience, and sustain well-being while working remotely. With proactive self-care and access to supportive resources, remote workers can thrive professionally and maintain a healthy work-life balance.

Building a Remote Team: Best Practices for Managers and Leaders

Building and managing a remote team requires strategic planning, effective communication, and strong leadership. This chapter explores best practices for managers and leaders to successfully hire and onboard remote employees, foster team collaboration, and manage performance and productivity.

Hiring and Onboarding Remote Employees

Hiring and onboarding remote employees requires a structured approach to ensure they feel welcomed, informed, and integrated into the team from the outset. Here's how managers and leaders can effectively manage this process:

1. Define Remote Role Requirements: Clearly outline the job responsibilities, skills, and qualifications needed for remote positions. Tailor job descriptions to reflect remote work expectations, including communication skills, self-motivation, and proficiency with remote collaboration tools.

2. Leverage Remote Hiring Tools: Utilize video interviews, online assessments, and virtual hiring platforms to evaluate candidates remotely. Assess candidates for their ability to thrive in a remote work environment, including their communication style and time management skills.

3. Communicate Transparently: Maintain open and transparent communication with candidates throughout the hiring process. Provide clear timelines, expectations, and next steps to ensure a positive candidate experience.

4. Facilitate Virtual Onboarding: Develop a comprehensive onboarding process that introduces remote employees to company culture, policies, and team dynamics. Provide access to necessary tools, resources, and training materials to support their transition into the role.

5. Assign a Buddy or Mentor: Pair new remote employees with a buddy or mentor who can offer guidance, answer questions, and facilitate introductions to team members. Encourage regular check-ins to ensure new hires feel supported and integrated.

6. Clarify Performance Expectations: Set clear performance goals, milestones, and expectations for remote employees from the outset. Align objectives with team and organizational priorities to establish accountability and foster motivation.

7. Collect Feedback: Solicit feedback from new hires about their onboarding experience to identify areas for improvement. Use feedback to refine the onboarding process and enhance future employee transitions.

Fostering Team Collaboration

Effective team collaboration is essential for remote teams to achieve collective goals, share knowledge, and maintain cohesion. Managers and leaders can foster collaboration through the following strategies:

1. Utilize Collaboration Tools: Implement reliable communication and collaboration tools, such as Slack, Microsoft Teams, or Zoom, to facilitate real-time communication, file sharing, and virtual meetings. Ensure team members are trained in using these tools effectively.

2. Establish Communication Norms: Define clear communication norms, including response times, preferred channels for different types of communication, and expectations for availability during work hours. Foster an environment where team members feel comfortable asking questions and sharing ideas.

3. Encourage Regular Meetings: Schedule regular team meetings, one-on-one check-ins, and project updates to maintain alignment and foster collaboration. Use video conferencing for face-to-face interactions that promote engagement and build rapport.

4. Promote Knowledge Sharing: Create opportunities for knowledge sharing and collaboration through virtual brainstorming sessions, peer reviews, and cross-functional projects. Encourage team members to leverage their diverse skills and perspectives to solve challenges collectively.

5. Cultivate a Team Culture: Cultivate a strong team culture based on trust, respect, and inclusivity. Celebrate achievements, recognize contributions, and encourage camaraderie through virtual team-building activities and social events.

6. Facilitate Virtual Team Bonding: Organize virtual social events, such as virtual coffee breaks, team lunches, or online games, to foster social connections and strengthen team cohesion. These activities help mitigate feelings of isolation and build a sense of community.

7. Clarify Roles and Responsibilities: Clearly define roles, responsibilities, and project ownership within the team. Ensure each team member understands their contribution to team goals and how their work aligns with broader organizational objectives.

Managing Performance and Productivity

Managing performance and productivity in a remote setting requires a results-oriented approach, effective communication, and regular performance assessments. Here's how managers and leaders can optimize performance management for remote teams:

1. Set Clear Goals and Expectations: Establish SMART goals (Specific, Measurable, Achievable, Relevant, Time-bound) that align with team and organizational objectives. Communicate performance expectations, deadlines, and deliverables to remote team members.

2. Implement Performance Metrics: Define key performance indicators (KPIs) and metrics to track individual and team performance remotely. Use data-driven insights to assess progress, identify areas for improvement, and recognize high-performing employees.

3. Provide Regular Feedback: Offer constructive feedback and recognition to remote team members on their performance and achievements. Schedule regular check-ins and performance reviews to discuss goals, challenges, and development opportunities.

4. Encourage Self-Assessment: Encourage remote employees to conduct self-assessments of their performance, strengths, and areas for growth. Self-assessment promotes accountability and empowers individuals to take ownership of their professional development.

5. Offer Professional Development: Support continuous learning and skill development through online training programs, certifications, and workshops. Invest in resources that enhance remote employees' competencies and career growth within the organization.

6. Promote Accountability: Foster a culture of accountability by holding remote team members responsible for their commitments and outcomes. Encourage autonomy, problem-solving, and proactive communication to drive results.

7. Address Performance Challenges: Address performance challenges promptly and constructively. Provide coaching, mentoring, or additional resources to support remote employees in overcoming obstacles and achieving performance goals.

Conclusion

Building and managing a remote team requires intentional efforts to hire and onboard effectively, foster collaboration, and optimize performance and productivity. By implementing best practices for remote team management, managers and leaders can create a supportive and productive work environment. These strategies promote communication, cohesion, and accountability among remote team members, ultimately contributing to organizational success and employee satisfaction. With a focus on leadership, communication, and continuous improvement, remote teams can thrive and achieve shared goals in a dynamic work environment.

Networking Remotely: Building Professional Relationships from Afar

Networking remotely is essential for professionals to expand their connections, build relationships, and advance their careers in a digital age. This chapter explores strategies for networking effectively from afar, including virtual networking strategies, participating in online communities, and leveraging social media platforms.

Virtual Networking Strategies

Virtual networking allows professionals to connect with peers, industry experts, and potential collaborators without geographical limitations. Here are effective strategies for networking remotely:

1. Attend Virtual Events and Webinars: Participate in online conferences, webinars, and virtual networking events related to your industry or professional interests. Engage in discussions, ask questions, and follow up with speakers or participants to expand your network.

2. Join Virtual Networking Platforms: Utilize professional networking platforms like LinkedIn, Meetup, or industry-specific forums to connect with like-minded professionals. Create a compelling profile that highlights your skills, experiences, and career goals to attract potential connections.

3. Schedule Virtual Coffee Meetings: Initiate virtual coffee meetings or informational interviews with contacts in your network. Use video conferencing tools to establish a personal connection, discuss shared interests, and explore potential collaboration opportunities.

4. Participate in Virtual Workshops or Training: Enroll in online workshops, training programs, or skill-building courses that offer networking opportunities. Engage with instructors, peers, and industry leaders to exchange ideas and build relationships.

5. Join Virtual Networking Groups: Join virtual networking groups or online communities focused on specific industries, professions, or career interests. Contribute to discussions, share insights, and connect with professionals who share similar career aspirations.

6. Organize Virtual Networking Sessions: Host virtual networking sessions or informal meetups with colleagues, alumni, or industry contacts. Facilitate introductions, encourage discussions on relevant topics, and foster connections among participants.

7. Follow Up and Stay Connected: After networking events or meetings, follow up promptly with new contacts via email or LinkedIn. Express appreciation for the conversation, reference key points discussed, and suggest ways to stay connected or collaborate in the future.

Participating in Online Communities

Online communities provide valuable platforms for professionals to engage in discussions, share knowledge, and establish credibility within their industries. Here's how to leverage online communities for networking:

1. Identify Relevant Communities: Identify online communities, forums, or discussion groups that align with your professional interests, career goals, or industry expertise. Choose communities known for active engagement and valuable content.

2. Contribute Thoughtfully: Actively participate in discussions by offering insights, sharing experiences, and asking thoughtful questions. Contribute valuable content that demonstrates your expertise and fosters meaningful interactions with other members.

3. Build Relationships: Establish connections with influential members or thought leaders within the online community. Follow their contributions, engage in conversations, and seek opportunities to collaborate or share resources.

4. Share Resources and Updates: Share relevant articles, industry news, or professional achievements with the online community. Position yourself as a resourceful and knowledgeable member who contributes to the community's growth and learning.

5. Seek Advice and Feedback: Use online communities to seek advice, feedback, or recommendations on professional challenges or career decisions. Leverage the collective expertise of community members to gain diverse perspectives and insights.

6. Attend Virtual Meetups or Events: Participate in virtual meetups, webinars, or networking events organized by online communities. Engage with fellow members in real-time discussions, network with new contacts, and strengthen existing relationships.

7. Maintain Professionalism: Maintain professionalism and respect community guidelines when interacting with members online. Demonstrate integrity, civility, and a willingness to contribute positively to discussions and community initiatives.

Leveraging Social Media

Social media platforms offer powerful tools for professionals to build their personal brand, showcase expertise, and connect with industry peers globally. Here's how to leverage social media for remote networking:

1. Optimize Your Profile: Create a professional profile on platforms like LinkedIn, Twitter, or Facebook that highlights your skills, experiences, and career accomplishments. Use a professional photo and craft a compelling bio that attracts connections.

2. Share Industry Insights: Share industry insights, trends, or thought leadership content on your social media profiles. Publish articles, blog posts, or updates that demonstrate your expertise and provide value to your network.

3. Engage with Content: Like, comment, and share posts from influencers, industry leaders, and peers in your network. Engage in conversations, offer perspectives, and build relationships with individuals who share common interests or career goals.

4. Join LinkedIn Groups: Join and participate in LinkedIn groups related to your profession, industry niche, or areas of expertise. Contribute to discussions, share relevant resources, and connect with group members to expand your network.

5. Utilize Hashtags: Use relevant hashtags on social media platforms to increase visibility and attract professionals interested in similar topics. Monitor trending hashtags and participate in conversations to enhance your online presence and reach new connections.

6. Network with Intention: Use direct messaging or InMail features on LinkedIn to initiate conversations with targeted connections. Personalize your messages, express genuine interest in their work, and propose ways to collaborate or share insights.

7. Monitor Analytics: Track engagement metrics, such as profile views, post interactions, and connection requests, using social media analytics tools. Evaluate the effectiveness of your networking efforts and adjust your strategy based on data insights.

Conclusion

Networking remotely requires proactive engagement, strategic communication, and effective leveraging of digital tools and platforms. By implementing virtual networking strategies, participating in online communities, and leveraging social media, professionals can expand their networks, build meaningful relationships, and advance their careers from afar. These practices promote professional growth, knowledge sharing, and collaboration in a globalized and interconnected professional landscape. With a dedication to building relationships and fostering connections, remote networking becomes a powerful tool for career development and long-term success.

Career Development: Advancing Your Career While Working from Home

Advancing your career while working from home requires proactive strategies, continuous learning, and strategic networking. This chapter explores key practices for setting career goals, pursuing professional development opportunities, and seeking mentorship and guidance to achieve career advancement in a remote work environment.

Setting Career Goals

Setting clear and achievable career goals is essential for career advancement and personal growth. Here's how to set effective career goals while working from home:

1. Reflect on Your Career Path: Take time to reflect on your current role, skills, strengths, and areas for growth. Consider your long-term career aspirations and where you envision yourself in the future.

2. Define SMART Goals: Establish SMART goals (Specific, Measurable, Achievable, Relevant, Time-bound) that align with your career objectives. Break down large goals into smaller, actionable steps to maintain focus and track progress.

3. Align Goals with Organizational Objectives: Ensure your career goals align with the priorities and objectives of your organization or team. Identify opportunities to contribute to company initiatives and demonstrate your value as a remote employee.

4. Create a Career Development Plan: Develop a career development plan outlining short-term and long-term goals, milestones, and timelines. Include strategies for acquiring new skills, expanding your knowledge base, and achieving career advancement.

5. Review and Adjust Goals Regularly: Regularly review your career goals to assess progress, identify challenges, and make necessary adjustments. Adapt goals based on changing priorities, professional interests, or opportunities that arise.

6. Seek Feedback: Solicit feedback from supervisors, mentors, or colleagues on your career goals and performance. Use feedback to gain insights, refine goals, and enhance your professional development strategy.

7. Stay Motivated and Accountable: Maintain motivation by celebrating achievements, staying committed to your goals, and holding yourself accountable for progress. Set deadlines, prioritize tasks, and seek support when needed to stay on track.

Pursuing Professional Development

Continuous learning and skill development are crucial for staying competitive and advancing your career while working remotely. Here's how to pursue professional development opportunities effectively:

1. Identify Skill Gaps: Assess your current skills and identify areas where additional training or development is needed. Consider skills relevant to your current role, emerging industry trends, or future career aspirations.

2. Take Online Courses and Workshops: Enroll in online courses, webinars, or virtual workshops that enhance your technical skills, industry knowledge, or leadership capabilities. Platforms like Coursera, Udemy, or LinkedIn Learning offer a wide range of courses.

3. Earn Certifications: Obtain industry certifications or credentials that validate your expertise and demonstrate your commitment to professional growth. Research certifications relevant to your field and career goals to enhance your qualifications.

4. Attend Virtual Conferences and Events: Participate in virtual conferences, seminars, or industry events to stay updated on industry trends, best practices, and networking opportunities. Engage with speakers, exhibitors, and attendees to expand your professional network.

5. Join Professional Associations: Become a member of professional associations or organizations related to your industry or field of expertise. Access resources, networking events, and educational opportunities that support your career development.

6. Participate in Cross-Functional Projects: Volunteer for cross-functional projects or initiatives within your organization to gain new experiences, build relationships with colleagues, and showcase your skills and capabilities.

7. Seek Feedback and Mentorship: Seek feedback from mentors, supervisors, or peers on your professional development goals and progress. Establish mentorship relationships with experienced professionals who can provide guidance, advice, and career support.

Seeking Mentorship and Guidance

Mentorship plays a critical role in career development by providing guidance, perspective, and support from experienced professionals. Here's how to seek mentorship effectively while working from home:

1. Identify Potential Mentors: Identify individuals within your organization, industry, or professional network who possess skills, knowledge, or experience aligned with your career goals. Look for mentors who can offer valuable insights and guidance.

2. Initiate Contact: Reach out to potential mentors via email, LinkedIn, or virtual networking platforms to express your interest in establishing a mentorship relationship. Clearly articulate your career goals, areas of interest, and reasons for seeking mentorship.

3. Schedule Virtual Meetings: Schedule virtual meetings or informational interviews with potential mentors to discuss your career aspirations, seek advice on professional challenges, and learn from their experiences. Prepare questions and topics for discussion to make the most of your meetings.

4. Be Open to Learning: Approach mentorship with an open mind and willingness to learn from your mentor's expertise and experiences. Be receptive to feedback, suggestions, and constructive criticism that contribute to your professional growth.

5. Set Goals for Mentorship: Establish specific goals and objectives for your mentorship relationship, such as acquiring new skills, expanding your network, or achieving career milestones. Collaborate with your mentor to create a plan for achieving these goals.

6. Seek Diverse Perspectives: Consider seeking mentorship from individuals with diverse backgrounds, perspectives, or career paths. Exposure to different viewpoints can broaden your understanding, challenge assumptions, and inspire innovative thinking.

7. Express Gratitude and Stay Connected: Show appreciation for your mentor's time, guidance, and support throughout your mentorship relationship. Stay connected by providing updates on your progress, seeking advice when needed, and maintaining professional rapport.

Conclusion

Advancing your career while working from home requires proactive career planning, continuous learning, and strategic networking. By setting clear career goals, pursuing professional development opportunities, and seeking mentorship and guidance, remote professionals can enhance their skills, expand their professional network, and achieve career advancement. These practices empower individuals to navigate remote work challenges, seize growth opportunities, and position themselves for success in a competitive job market. With dedication to professional development and ongoing self-improvement, remote workers can cultivate fulfilling careers and achieve their long-term career aspirations from any location.

Cybersecurity: Protecting Your Work and Personal Data

Cybersecurity is critical for remote workers to safeguard their work-related and personal information from online threats and vulnerabilities. This chapter explores strategies for understanding cyber threats, implementing security measures, and adopting best practices to enhance cybersecurity while working remotely.

Understanding Cyber Threats

Understanding the types of cyber threats that remote workers may encounter is essential for mitigating risks and protecting sensitive data. Common cyber threats include:

1. Phishing Attacks: Phishing involves fraudulent emails, messages, or websites designed to deceive individuals into providing sensitive information such as passwords or financial details. Remote workers should be cautious of suspicious emails or links.

2. Malware and Ransomware: Malware is malicious software designed to disrupt, damage, or gain unauthorized access to computer systems. Ransomware encrypts files and demands payment for decryption, posing a significant threat to data security.

3. Social Engineering: Social engineering tactics exploit human psychology to manipulate individuals into divulging confidential information or performing actions that compromise security. Examples include pretexting and baiting.

4. Unsecured Wi-Fi Networks: Connecting to unsecured or public Wi-Fi networks exposes remote workers to potential eavesdropping and data interception by cyber criminals. Use virtual private networks (VPNs) for secure data transmission.

5. Weak Passwords and Authentication: Weak passwords or reuse of passwords across multiple accounts increase vulnerability to unauthorized access. Implement strong, unique passwords and enable multi-factor authentication (MFA) for enhanced security.

6. Insider Threats: Insider threats involve unauthorized or malicious actions by individuals within an organization, such as data theft or sabotage. Implement access controls and monitor privileged user activities to mitigate insider risks.

7. Outdated Software and Patch Management: Failure to update software and apply security patches leaves systems vulnerable to exploitation by cyber attackers. Regularly update operating systems, applications, and security software to mitigate vulnerabilities.

Implementing Security Measures

Implementing robust security measures is crucial for protecting work-related and personal data from cyber threats. Consider the following cybersecurity practices:

1. Use Secure Passwords: Create strong, complex passwords that combine uppercase and lowercase letters, numbers, and special characters. Avoid using easily guessable information and update passwords regularly.

2. Enable Multi-Factor Authentication (MFA): Enable MFA for accessing accounts and systems to add an extra layer of security. MFA requires users to verify their identity using multiple factors, such as passwords and biometric verification.

3. Secure Network Connections: Use VPNs when accessing corporate networks or sensitive information over public or unsecured Wi-Fi networks. VPNs encrypt data transmitted between devices and remote servers, protecting against interception.

4. Install and Update Security Software: Install reputable antivirus software, firewalls, and anti-malware programs on all devices. Keep security software up to date to defend against evolving threats and vulnerabilities.

5. Backup Data Regularly: Regularly backup work-related and personal data to secure cloud storage or external devices. Backup copies enable data recovery in case of ransomware attacks, hardware failures, or data loss incidents.

6. Implement Encryption: Encrypt sensitive data both at rest (stored data) and in transit (data transmitted over networks). Encryption converts data into unreadable ciphertext that can only be decrypted with authorized access.

7. Educate and Train Employees: Provide cybersecurity awareness training to remote workers on recognizing phishing attempts, secure password practices, and safe browsing habits. Empower employees to identify and report suspicious activities promptly.

Best Practices for Remote Workers

Adopting best practices enhances cybersecurity posture and reduces the risk of cyber threats for remote workers. Follow these best practices:

1. Be Vigilant Against Phishing: Verify the authenticity of emails, links, or attachments before clicking or providing sensitive information. Report suspicious emails to IT security immediately.

2. Secure Devices and Workspaces: Lock devices when not in use and store them in secure locations. Avoid leaving devices unattended in public places or vehicles where they can be easily stolen.

3. Update Software Regularly: Enable automatic updates for operating systems, applications, and security patches to address vulnerabilities promptly. Regular updates enhance device security and protect against exploits.

4. Limit Access and Use Strong Authentication: Restrict access to sensitive information based on job responsibilities. Implement strong authentication methods, such as biometrics or tokens, for accessing critical systems or data.

5. Monitor Accounts and Statements: Regularly monitor bank accounts, credit card statements, and online accounts for unauthorized transactions or suspicious activity. Report any discrepancies to financial institutions or service providers immediately.

6. Backup Important Data: Maintain backups of critical work-related and personal data to ensure data recovery in case of data loss incidents or ransomware attacks. Store backups securely and test restoration procedures periodically.

7. Report Security Incidents: Promptly report suspected security incidents, data breaches, or unusual activities to IT support or cybersecurity teams. Follow organizational protocols for incident response and data breach notifications.

Conclusion

Cybersecurity is paramount for remote workers to protect their work-related and personal data from cyber threats and vulnerabilities. By understanding cyber threats, implementing security measures, and adopting best practices, remote workers can enhance their cybersecurity posture and mitigate risks effectively. Proactive security measures, regular updates, and cybersecurity awareness empower individuals to maintain confidentiality, integrity, and availability of information in a remote work environment. With diligence and adherence to cybersecurity guidelines, remote workers can navigate online threats and safeguard their digital assets with confidence.

Remote Work Tools: Software and Apps to Boost Productivity

Remote work tools play a crucial role in facilitating collaboration, managing projects, and enhancing productivity for remote teams. This chapter explores various software and apps designed to streamline workflows, improve communication, and optimize remote work efficiency.

Project Management Tools

Project management tools enable remote teams to plan, organize, and track tasks, projects, and deadlines effectively. Key features typically include task assignment, progress tracking, milestone management, and team collaboration. Popular project management tools include:

1. Trello: A visual project management tool that uses boards, lists, and cards to organize tasks and workflows. Teams can customize boards, assign tasks, set deadlines, and track progress in real time.

2. Asana: A versatile project management platform that allows teams to create projects, assign tasks, set priorities, and visualize project timelines using Kanban boards or task lists. Asana integrates with various third-party apps to streamline workflows.

3. Monday.com: An intuitive platform for project tracking and collaboration, featuring customizable workflows, Gantt charts, and task dependencies. Teams can manage projects, allocate resources, and monitor progress from a centralized dashboard.

4. Jira: Ideal for software development teams, Jira offers agile project management capabilities, including sprint planning, issue tracking, and release management. It supports collaboration through customizable workflows and integrations with development tools.

5. Basecamp: A user-friendly project management tool that combines project planning, task management, file storage, and team communication in one platform. Basecamp features message boards, to-do lists, schedules, and document sharing for streamlined collaboration.

Time Tracking Software

Time tracking software helps remote workers monitor and manage their time effectively, ensuring productivity and accountability. These tools track hours worked, measure task durations, and generate reports for project billing or performance analysis. Popular time-tracking software includes:

1. Toggl: A simple time-tracking app that allows users to track time spent on tasks, projects, or clients. Toggl offers integrations with various project management tools and generates detailed reports for analysis and invoicing.

2. Clockify A free time tracking tool with features for tracking billable hours, generating timesheets, and analyzing productivity trends. Clockify supports team collaboration and integrates with popular productivity apps for seamless workflow management.

3. Harvest: An intuitive time tracking and invoicing tool that helps remote teams track billable hours, manage expenses, and create detailed reports. Harvest integrates with project management platforms and accounting software for streamlined project tracking and financial management.

4. RescueTime: A productivity monitoring tool that tracks time spent on websites, apps, and tasks to provide insights into daily productivity habits. RescueTime offers goal setting, distraction blocking, and productivity reports to optimize time management.

5. Hubstaff: A comprehensive time tracking and employee monitoring software that tracks work hours, activity levels, and project progress. Hubstaff offers GPS tracking, screenshots, and payroll integrations for remote team management and accountability.

Collaboration Platforms

Collaboration platforms facilitate real-time communication, file sharing, and team collaboration for remote teams. These tools promote seamless information exchange, project coordination, and virtual meetings. Popular collaboration platforms include:

1. Slack: A messaging app for teams that enables instant messaging, file sharing, and channel-based communication. Slack integrates with productivity tools, supports voice and video calls, and offers customizable notifications for efficient team collaboration.

2. Microsoft Teams: A unified communication and collaboration platform within Microsoft 365, featuring chat, video meetings, file storage, and application integration. Teams allow for channel-based communication, document co-authoring, and virtual collaboration spaces.

3. Zoom: A video conferencing platform that facilitates virtual meetings, webinars, and online collaboration. Zoom offers HD video and audio, screen sharing, breakout rooms, and recording capabilities for remote team communication and collaboration.

4. Google Workspace (formerly G Suite): A suite of cloud-based productivity tools, including Gmail, Google Drive, Google Docs, and Google Meet, for real-time collaboration, document editing, and video conferencing. Google Workspace enhances team productivity through seamless integration and collaboration features.

5. Cisco Webex: A secure video conferencing and collaboration platform that supports virtual meetings, webinars, and team messaging. Webex offers screen sharing, whiteboarding, and integrations with productivity tools to enhance remote team collaboration and productivity.

Conclusion

Remote work tools empower teams to overcome geographical barriers, collaborate effectively, and maximize productivity in a virtual work environment. By leveraging project management tools, time-tracking software, and collaboration platforms, remote teams can streamline workflows, track progress, and communicate seamlessly across locations. These tools enhance task management, facilitate real-time communication, and support remote team collaboration through integrated features and intuitive interfaces. With a focus on efficiency, transparency, and communication, remote work tools enable organizations to adapt to remote work trends and achieve operational success in a digital-first workplace.

Case Studies: Success Stories from Remote Workers

Remote work has become a prominent feature of the modern professional landscape, offering flexibility and new opportunities for individuals and organizations. This chapter explores success stories from remote workers, featuring interviews with remote work pioneers, lessons learned from successful remote teams, and inspiring stories and tips to help others thrive in a remote work environment.

Interviews with Remote Work Pioneers

Remote work pioneers are individuals who have successfully navigated and excelled in remote work long before it became mainstream. Their experiences offer valuable insights into the strategies and practices that contribute to remote work success.

Interview with Sarah Johnson, Freelance Graphic Designer

Background: Sarah Johnson has been a freelance graphic designer for over a decade. She transitioned to remote work early in her career to gain more control over her schedule and work-life balance.

Key Takeaways:
1. Embrace Flexibility: Sarah values the flexibility that remote work offers, allowing her to work during her most productive hours and balance personal commitments.
2. Build a Strong Portfolio: A comprehensive and visually appealing portfolio has been crucial for attracting clients and showcasing her skills.
3. Network Actively: Sarah emphasizes the importance of networking through online platforms, industry forums, and virtual events to build connections and secure freelance projects.
4. Invest in Professional Development: Continuous learning through online courses and workshops has helped Sarah stay updated with design trends and software advancements.

Interview with David Lee, Remote Software Engineer

Background: David Lee transitioned to remote work five years ago when his company adopted a remote-first policy. He enjoys the autonomy and flexibility that remote work provides.

Key Takeaways:
1. Effective Communication: David highlights the importance of clear and frequent communication with team members and supervisors to ensure alignment and progress.
2. Time Management: Using time management tools and techniques, such as the Pomodoro Technique, has helped David maintain productivity and avoid burnout.

3. Remote Collaboration Tools: Leveraging collaboration tools like Slack, Jira, and Zoom has facilitated seamless coordination and teamwork with colleagues across different time zones.
4. Work-Life Balance: Establishing a dedicated workspace and setting boundaries has been essential for David to maintain a healthy work-life balance.

Lessons Learned from Successful Remote Teams

Successful remote teams demonstrate how collaboration, communication, and culture can thrive in a remote environment. Here are key lessons learned from their experiences.

Lesson 1: Foster a Strong Team Culture

Example: Buffer, a social media management company, operates as a fully remote team. They prioritize building a strong team culture through transparent communication, regular virtual meetups, and team-building activities.

Key Takeaways:
1. Transparency: Sharing company goals, performance metrics, and decision-making processes openly fosters trust and alignment among team members.
2. Regular Check-ins: Weekly team meetings and one-on-one check-ins help maintain connection, address challenges, and celebrate achievements.
3. Team-Building Activities: Virtual team-building activities, such as online games, virtual coffee breaks, and team retreats, strengthen relationships and boost morale.

Lesson 2: Prioritize Communication and Collaboration

Example: GitLab, a fully remote software development company, emphasizes the importance of communication and collaboration through detailed documentation and asynchronous communication practices.

Key Takeaways:
1. Documentation: Comprehensive documentation of processes, projects, and workflows ensures that team members have access to information and can work independently.
2. Asynchronous Communication: Embracing asynchronous communication allows team members to collaborate across different time zones and reduces the need for constant real-time meetings.
3. Collaboration Tools: Using integrated collaboration tools like GitLab, Slack, and Google Workspace enhances coordination and productivity.

Lesson 3: Invest in Employee Well-being

Example: Automattic, the company behind WordPress.com, places a strong emphasis on employee well-being by offering flexible work schedules, wellness programs, and professional development opportunities.

Key Takeaways:
1. Flexible Work Schedules: Allowing employees to choose their work hours based on their personal preferences and peak productivity times promotes work-life balance.
2. Wellness Programs: Providing access to mental health resources, fitness programs, and wellness stipends supports employees' physical and mental well-being.
3. Professional Development: Encouraging continuous learning through courses, workshops, and conferences helps employees grow and stay engaged.

Inspiring Stories and Tips

Inspiring stories from remote workers highlight the diverse ways individuals have leveraged remote work to achieve personal and professional success. Here are some notable examples and tips.

Story 1: Maria Sanchez, Digital Nomad and Content Writer

Background: Maria Sanchez left her corporate job to become a digital nomad and pursue her passion for travel and writing. She has visited over 30 countries while working remotely as a content writer.

Inspiring Tips:
1. Leverage Freelance Platforms: Platforms like Upwork, Fiverr, and Freelancer provide opportunities to secure remote writing gigs and build a client base.
2. Maintain a Routine: Establishing a daily routine that includes dedicated work hours, exercise, and leisure activities helps Maria stay productive and balanced.
3. Embrace New Cultures: Immersing herself in different cultures has enriched Maria's writing and broadened her perspective.

Story 2: John Miller, Remote Marketing Consultant

Background: John Miller transitioned from a traditional office role to a remote marketing consultant to spend more time with his family. He successfully built a remote consultancy business by leveraging his marketing expertise.

Inspiring Tips:
1. Build an Online Presence: Creating a professional website and leveraging social media to showcase expertise and attract clients has been crucial for John's consultancy business.
2. Client Communication: Maintaining regular communication with clients through video calls, emails, and project management tools ensures transparency and client satisfaction.
3. Continuous Learning: Staying updated with marketing trends and tools through online courses and industry webinars has helped John deliver value to his clients.

Story 3: Emily Chen, Remote Customer Support Specialist

Background: Emily Chen switched to remote work to achieve a better work-life balance and reduce commute stress. She excels as a remote customer support specialist for a global tech company.

Inspiring Tips:
1. Organize Your Workspace: Creating a comfortable and organized workspace free from distractions enhances Emily's focus and efficiency.
2. Develop Soft Skills: Effective communication, empathy, and problem-solving skills are essential for providing excellent customer support remotely.
3. Utilize Support Tools: Leveraging customer support tools like Zendesk, Freshdesk, and Intercom streamlines Emily's workflow and improves response times.

Conclusion

Success stories from remote workers demonstrate that with the right strategies, tools, and mindset, remote work can lead to significant personal and professional achievements. Interviews with remote work pioneers, lessons learned from successful remote teams, and inspiring stories provide valuable insights and practical tips for navigating and excelling in a remote work environment. By embracing flexibility, prioritizing communication, investing in professional development, and maintaining a healthy work-life balance, remote workers can achieve their goals and thrive in a dynamic and evolving work landscape.

Future Trends: The Evolving Landscape of Remote Work

The landscape of remote work continues to evolve, driven by technological advancements, shifting organizational policies, and changing employee expectations. This chapter explores emerging technologies, the future of remote work policies, and predictions and trends that will shape the future of remote work.

Emerging Technologies

Emerging technologies are playing a crucial role in transforming remote work, making it more efficient, secure, and collaborative. Here are some key technologies that are shaping the future of remote work:

1. Artificial Intelligence (AI) and Machine Learning

AI and machine learning are enhancing remote work by automating routine tasks, improving decision-making, and providing personalized experiences. Key applications include:

- Chatbots and Virtual Assistants: AI-powered chatbots and virtual assistants streamline customer support, handle repetitive queries, and assist with administrative tasks.
- Predictive Analytics: Machine learning algorithms analyze data to forecast trends, optimize workflows, and enhance productivity.
- Personalized Learning: AI-driven platforms offer customized training and development programs tailored to individual needs and career goals.

2. Virtual Reality (VR) and Augmented Reality (AR)

VR and AR technologies are revolutionizing remote collaboration, training, and immersive experiences. Key applications include:

- Virtual Meetings and Collaboration: VR and AR platforms create virtual meeting spaces where remote teams can interact, brainstorm, and collaborate in a more immersive environment.
- Training and Simulation: VR and AR provide realistic simulations for training purposes, allowing employees to practice skills in a safe and controlled setting.
- Remote Assistance: AR enables remote experts to provide real-time guidance and support by overlaying digital information onto physical environments.

3. Cloud Computing

Cloud computing continues to be a cornerstone of remote work, enabling access to data, applications, and services from anywhere. Key benefits include:

- Scalability: Cloud platforms allow organizations to scale their IT resources up or down based on demand, ensuring flexibility and cost-efficiency.
- Collaboration: Cloud-based tools facilitate real-time collaboration, file sharing, and project management for remote teams.
- Data Security: Advanced cloud security measures, such as encryption and access controls, protect sensitive information and ensure compliance with data privacy regulations.

4. 5G Connectivity

The rollout of 5G networks promises to significantly enhance remote work by providing faster and more reliable internet connectivity. Key advantages include:

- Improved Video Conferencing: High-speed 5G networks enable seamless high-definition video calls with minimal latency.
- Enhanced Mobility: Remote workers can access data and applications on the go without compromising speed or performance.
- IoT Integration: 5G facilitates the integration of Internet of Things (IoT) devices, enabling remote monitoring and control of smart office environments.

The Future of Remote Work Policies

The future of remote work policies will be shaped by a combination of organizational needs, employee preferences, and societal trends. Here are some key considerations:

1. Hybrid Work Models

Many organizations are adopting hybrid work models that combine remote and in-office work. Key features of hybrid models include:

- Flexibility: Employees have the flexibility to choose where they work based on their tasks, preferences, and personal circumstances.
- Office Hubs: Companies maintain office hubs for collaborative work, meetings, and team-building activities while allowing remote work for individual tasks.
- Dynamic Policies: Organizations develop dynamic remote work policies that can adapt to changing conditions and employee needs.

2. Focus on Results and Outcomes

Future remote work policies will emphasize outcomes and results rather than hours worked. Key aspects include:

- Performance Metrics: Clear performance metrics and key performance indicators (KPIs) are established to measure productivity and success.
- Autonomy: Employees are given greater autonomy and trust to manage their work, fostering a results-oriented culture.
- Accountability: Transparent accountability mechanisms ensure that goals and deadlines are met without micromanagement.

3. Employee Well-being and Work-Life Balance

Organizations will prioritize employee well-being and work-life balance in their remote work policies. Key initiatives include:

- Mental Health Support: Providing access to mental health resources, counseling services, and wellness programs to support employee well-being.
- Flexible Schedules: Allowing flexible work schedules to accommodate personal commitments, caregiving responsibilities, and individual preferences.
- Burnout Prevention: Implementing measures to prevent burnout, such as encouraging regular breaks, promoting healthy work habits, and monitoring workload.

Predictions and Trends

Several predictions and trends will influence the future of remote work. Here are some notable ones:

1. Increased Adoption of Remote Work

The trend towards remote work is expected to continue growing as more organizations recognize the benefits of flexibility, cost savings, and access to a global talent pool. Predictions include:

- Permanent Remote Work Options: More companies will offer permanent remote work options to attract and retain top talent.
- Global Talent Acquisition: Organizations will expand their talent search beyond geographic boundaries, hiring skilled professionals from around the world.
- Reduced Office Footprint: Companies will reduce their physical office space, investing in technology and infrastructure to support remote work.

2. Evolving Collaboration Tools

Collaboration tools will continue to evolve to meet the needs of remote teams. Predictions include:

- Integrated Platforms: Unified platforms that combine communication, project management, and collaboration tools into a single interface.
- Enhanced Security: Improved security features, such as end-to-end encryption and biometric authentication, to protect sensitive information.
- AI-Powered Collaboration: AI-driven features, such as smart scheduling, automated task assignment, and real-time language translation, enhance collaboration efficiency.

3. Focus on Cybersecurity

As remote work becomes more prevalent, cybersecurity will remain a top priority. Predictions include:

- Zero Trust Security Models: Organizations will adopt zero trust security models that require continuous verification of users and devices.
- Advanced Threat Detection: AI and machine learning will be used to detect and respond to cyber threats in real time.
- Employee Training: Ongoing cybersecurity training and awareness programs will be essential to mitigate risks and protect against cyber attacks.

Conclusion

The future of remote work is shaped by emerging technologies, evolving organizational policies, and trends that prioritize flexibility, collaboration, and employee well-being. By embracing these changes and adopting innovative tools and practices, organizations can create a dynamic and productive remote work environment that meets the needs of both employees and businesses. As the remote work landscape continues to evolve, staying informed about technological advancements and policy trends will be crucial for success in the digital age.

Conclusion: Embracing the Remote Work Revolution

As we conclude our comprehensive guide on remote work, it's important to revisit the key points we've covered, offer encouragement for those embarking on or continuing their remote work journey, and share some final thoughts on the future of this dynamic work model. Remote work is not just a temporary trend; it is a transformative shift in how we approach our professional lives. Understanding its nuances, leveraging its benefits, and preparing for its challenges are essential for success.

Recap of Key Points

Throughout this book, we have delved into various aspects of remote work, from setting up your home office to mastering time management and utilizing productivity tools. Here is a recap of the key points discussed:

1. Setting Up Your Home Office: Essentials for Success
  - Choosing the Right Space: Selecting a quiet, dedicated space in your home that minimizes distractions is crucial. Invest in ergonomic furniture and ensure good lighting.
  - Essential Equipment and Tools: A reliable computer, high-speed internet, and necessary peripherals like a webcam and headset are vital. Additionally, software tools for communication and collaboration are essential.
  - Ergonomics and Comfort: Prioritize ergonomics by using an adjustable chair, and a desk at the correct height, and positioning your monitor at eye level to prevent strain and injury.

2. Time Management: Strategies for a Structured Workday
  - Creating a Daily Routine: Establishing a consistent daily schedule helps maintain productivity and work-life balance. Include breaks and time for physical activity.
  - Prioritizing Tasks: Use methods like the Eisenhower Matrix or the ABCDE method to prioritize tasks based on urgency and importance.
  - Avoiding Procrastination: Techniques such as the Pomodoro Technique can help maintain focus and manage time effectively.

3. Communication Tools: Staying Connected and Collaborative
  - Video Conferencing Platforms: Tools like Zoom, Microsoft Teams, and Google Meet facilitate virtual meetings and collaboration.
  - Messaging and Collaboration Tools: Slack, Trello, and Asana are excellent for team communication and project management.
  - Effective Communication Practices: Clear, concise communication and regular updates are key to successful remote teamwork.

4. Work-Life Balance: Maintaining Boundaries in a Remote Environment
    - Setting Boundaries with Family and Friends: Establish clear boundaries to minimize interruptions during work hours.
    - Taking Breaks and Avoiding Burnout: Regular breaks and mindfulness practices can prevent burnout and maintain mental well-being.
    - Creating a Healthy Work-Life Balance: Define distinct work and personal time to maintain a balanced lifestyle.

5. Productivity Hacks: Techniques to Maximize Efficiency
    - Time Blocking and Scheduling: Allocate specific time blocks for different tasks to maintain focus and productivity.
    - The Pomodoro Technique: Work in short, focused intervals with breaks to sustain high levels of productivity.
    - Minimizing Distractions: Identify and eliminate common distractions to create a conducive work environment.

6. Overcoming Remote Work Challenges: Common Pitfalls and Solutions
    - Dealing with Isolation and Loneliness: Stay connected with colleagues and engage in social activities outside of work.
    - Managing Technical Issues: Ensure you have a reliable technical setup and access to IT support.
    - Staying Motivated: Set clear goals, reward yourself, and stay connected with your team to maintain motivation.

7. Mental Health: Staying Positive and Focused While Working Remotely
    - Practicing Mindfulness and Meditation: Incorporate mindfulness practices into your routine to manage stress and enhance focus.
    - Seeking Support and Counseling: Access mental health resources and support when needed.
    - Maintaining Physical Health: Regular exercise, a healthy diet, and adequate sleep are crucial for overall well-being.

8. Building a Remote Team: Best Practices for Managers and Leaders
    - Hiring and Onboarding Remote Employees: Develop a robust hiring process and provide comprehensive onboarding to integrate new hires.
    - Fostering Team Collaboration: Encourage collaboration through regular virtual meetings and team-building activities.
    - Managing Performance and Productivity: Use clear metrics and regular feedback to manage performance and productivity effectively.

9. Networking Remotely: Building Professional Relationships from Afar
    - Virtual Networking Strategies: Participate in virtual events and use online platforms to network professionally.

- Participating in Online Communities: Engage in online communities related to your industry to build connections.
- Leveraging Social Media: Use social media to showcase your expertise and connect with peers.

10. Career Development: Advancing Your Career While Working from Home
- Setting Career Goals: Define clear, achievable career goals and create a plan to achieve them.
- Pursuing Professional Development: Invest in continuous learning through online courses and certifications.
- Seeking Mentorship and Guidance: Find mentors and seek guidance to advance your career.

11. Cybersecurity: Protecting Your Work and Personal Data
- Understanding Cyber Threats: Stay informed about common cyber threats and how to protect against them.
- Implementing Security Measures: Use strong passwords, enable two-factor authentication, and keep software updated.
- Best Practices for Remote Workers: Follow best practices like using VPNs and secure networks to safeguard data.

12. Remote Work Tools: Software and Apps to Boost Productivity
- Project Management Tools: Tools like Asana, Trello, and Monday.com help manage projects and tasks effectively.
- Time Tracking Software: Time tracking apps like Toggl and Harvest help monitor productivity and manage time.
- Collaboration Platforms: Platforms like Slack, Microsoft Teams, and Google Workspace facilitate seamless collaboration.

13. Case Studies: Success Stories from Remote Workers
- Interviews with Remote Work Pioneers: Learn from the experiences of successful remote workers.
- Lessons Learned from Successful Remote Teams: Discover best practices from high-performing remote teams.
- Inspiring Stories and Tips: Gain inspiration and practical tips from remote work success stories.

14. Future Trends: The Evolving Landscape of Remote Work
- Emerging Technologies: Explore how AI, VR, AR, cloud computing, and 5G are shaping the future of remote work.
- The Future of Remote Work Policies: Understand the evolving nature of remote work policies and hybrid work models.
- Predictions and Trends: Stay informed about trends and predictions that will influence remote work.

Encouragement for the Future

Embracing remote work requires adaptability, resilience, and a proactive approach. Here are some key points of encouragement as you navigate the remote work landscape:

1. Embrace Change

Change is inevitable, and embracing it with a positive mindset can lead to growth and new opportunities. Remote work offers a unique chance to redefine your work-life balance, enhance productivity, and pursue personal and professional development. Be open to experimenting with new tools, techniques, and workflows that can improve your remote work experience.

2. Leverage Technology

Technology is a powerful enabler of remote work. Stay updated with the latest tools and technologies that can enhance your productivity and collaboration. Invest time in learning and mastering these tools to make the most of your remote work setup.

3. Prioritize Well-being

Your well-being is paramount. Make time for physical activity, mental health practices, and social connections. A healthy work-life balance is essential for sustained productivity and job satisfaction. Don't hesitate to seek support and resources when needed.

4. Stay Connected

Human connection is vital, even in a remote work environment. Make an effort to stay connected with colleagues, friends, and family. Regular communication and social interactions can mitigate feelings of isolation and enhance your overall well-being.

5. Focus on Continuous Learning

Remote work offers flexibility, which can be leveraged to pursue continuous learning and professional development. Invest in online courses, certifications, and training programs that align with your career goals. Continuous learning can open up new opportunities and keep you competitive in the job market.

1

---

[1] Final Thoughts

Remote work is more than just a way to work; it is a revolution in how we approach our professional lives. It offers unparalleled flexibility, the opportunity for a better work-life balance, and the potential for increased productivity and job satisfaction. However, it also comes with challenges that require careful management and a proactive approach.

By understanding the essentials of setting up a home office, mastering time management, utilizing productivity tools, and prioritizing well-being, you can thrive in a remote work environment. Learning from the experiences of successful remote workers and staying informed about future trends can further enhance your remote work experience.

As we look to the future, the remote work revolution is set to continue evolving. Embrace the opportunities it offers, stay adaptable, and be proactive in managing the challenges. With the right strategies and mindset, remote work can lead to a fulfilling and successful professional journey. Whether you are just starting or have been working remotely for years, remember that you have the tools and resources to succeed. Here's to embracing the remote work revolution and thriving in this new era of work.

Max Fortune